THINK ABOUT

Being
BLIND

Peter White

First published in the UK in 1998 by
Belitha Press Limited
London House, Great Eastern Wharf,
Parkgate Road, London SW11 4NQ

Published in the United States by
Smart Apple Media
123 South Broad Street
Mankato, Minnesota 56001

Library of Congress Cataloging-in-Publication Data

White, Peter, 1947 June 18–
Being blind / Peter White.
p. cm. — (Think about)
Includes index.
Summary: Describes what it is like to be blind, some of the challenges faced by blind
people, and the ways they cope with everyday life.
ISBN 1-887068-84-8
1. Blindness—Juvenile literature.   [1. Blind.   2. Physically handicapped.]   I. Title.
II. Series: Think about (Mankato, Minn.)

HV1596.3.W55   1999
362.4'1—dc21   98-33995

9   8   7   6   5   4   3

Photographs by: Baum Elektronic, BBC Photographs, Bridgeman Art Library, Bibliothèque
Nationale, Brytech Inc., Christian Blind Mission, Clearvision, Collections, Anthea Sieveking,
Brian Shuel, Lesley Howling, Dee Conway, Mary Evans Picture Library, Eye Ubiquitous, Getty
Images, Andrea Booher, Tony Latham, Ken Fisher, Art Brewer, UHB Trust, Arthur Tilley, Alan
Levenson, Frank Ores, Penny Gentieu, Sally & Richard Greenhill, The Guide Dogs for the
Blind Association, Rebecca Harris, Image Bank, Jane Art, Imperial War Musuem, London
Metropolitan Archives, The Nottingham Group Ltd, Redferns, David Refern, Retrograph
Archive, RNIB, Isabel Lilly, Bob Kauders, Royal London Society for the Blind, Eric Richmond,
Spectrum Colour Library, Will & Deni McIntyre, Adam Hart Davis, Hank Morgan,
Stockmarket/Zefa, K & H Benser

Words in **bold** are explained in the glossary on pages 30 and 31.

ABOUT THE AUTHOR

Although Peter White has been blind all his life, his disability did not stop him from becoming a successful journalist, writer, and broadcaster. He has worked on many television and radio programs for the blind.

Contents

Understanding blindness

At some point, most children have tried wearing a blindfold. Most of them probably stumbled around, bumping into tables, walls, and other people. Blind people, on the other hand, have much more control as they move around. They quickly remember where things are and learn to be aware of objects around them.

Levels of blindness

Only one in five blind people can see nothing at all. Most blind people have some vision, even if it is only shadowy. They learn to use their limited vision and other senses so skillfully that few people realize how little they can see.

◀ The right-hand side of this photograph shows how the world looks to many people with damaged sight. This is a common form of blindness.

Everyday activities

To a person who suddenly lost his sight, many everyday things—finding clothes and getting dressed in the morning, for example—would be difficult. Blind people keep their clothes in separate drawers or in a certain order so they know exactly where everything is. Some totally blind people use their sense of touch to find or recognize things.

The sense of touch can be very useful to people who can see nothing at all.

THINK ABOUT

Meal time

If you were blind, how would you know what you were eating before you put it into your mouth? People with no sight at all use smell and touch to guess what's on their plate. Some people use the clock method; they imagine their plate is a clock and are told that pizza is at five o'clock, peas are at eight o'clock, and so on. Sometimes they just stick a fork in and hope for the best!

Keeping up with technology

Not all blind people have to miss out on television and movies. It is surprising how much they can figure out by listening carefully and using their limited sight and a bit of imagination. Computers can be **adapted** for blind people by having large print. Some computers speak or have a **Braille** printer. This **partially-sighted** boy can see bright shapes on the screen.

What is blindness?

A few people can see nothing at all, but most of the people we call blind can see a little. People with poor vision are called partially-sighted. Many people are **near-sighted** or **far-sighted**. Most kinds of blindness are more likely to affect people as they grow old, but disease or an accident can harm eyes at any time. Sometimes children are born blind or with very poor sight.

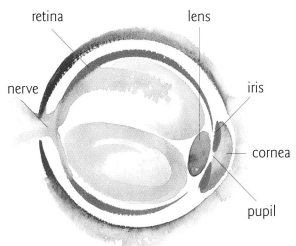

▼ **A human eye**

retina

lens

nerve

iris

cornea

pupil

How the eye works

The eye is like a camera. It takes a picture through the **lens** just like a camera does. The back of the eye is like the film where the photograph is stored. **Nerve** messages carry the picture to the brain. Any part of the eye can go wrong, which is why there are so many different levels of blindness.

Why do people go blind?

Cataracts are one of the most common causes of blindness. They usually affect adults, but children can get them too. Cataracts grow on the lens of the eye and make people feel as if they are looking through clouds. Part of the **retina** can also be damaged, preventing the person from seeing detail. Sometimes older people get a disease called **glaucoma**.

◄ **A boy at a school for blind children practices his handwriting. He makes the letters big so that he can see them clearly.**

Dangerous diseases

Illnesses such as **diabetes** and **AIDS** can affect many parts of the body, including the eyes. A lot of people in the world's poorer countries are blinded by diseases. In parts of Africa, a disease called river blindness is carried by a fly that lives near rivers. River blindness can cause whole villages of people to go blind.

This man has river blindness. A child acts as his eyes by leading him along. Many people in poor countries cannot afford an operation to save their sight.

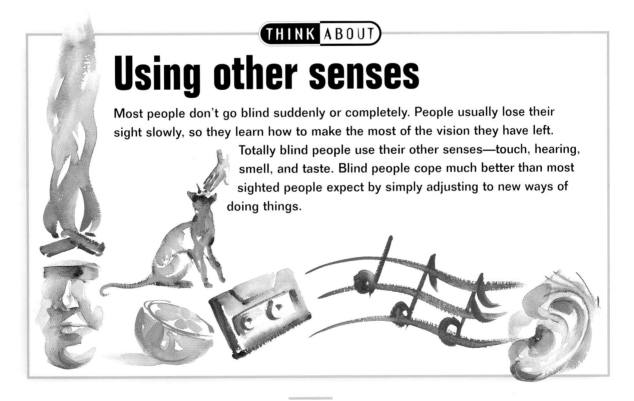

THINK ABOUT

Using other senses

Most people don't go blind suddenly or completely. People usually lose their sight slowly, so they learn how to make the most of the vision they have left. Totally blind people use their other senses—touch, hearing, smell, and taste. Blind people cope much better than most sighted people expect by simply adjusting to new ways of doing things.

Blindness over the years

Blindness has often puzzled and frightened people. Warriors such as the Spartans of ancient Greece thought that blind people could not serve a purpose in society because they couldn't fight. Babies who were born blind were left outside to die. Other people, such as the Romans, believed that blind people had special powers and that they could see into the future.

Treatment for blindness

One hundred years ago, people knew nothing about eyes and what could go wrong with them. They often believed that blindness was punishment for people who had done something bad. People who went blind were tricked into thinking that powders and potions would cure their blindness, when really they did no good at all.

Eye operations were painful and messy in the years before modern surgery. This drawing shows an eye operation in 18th-century France.

Learning and working

Most blind children were not educated, and they had to stay at home instead of going to school. Until the invention of the Braille system in 1824, they had no way of reading. Children who did go to school had to try to memorize their lessons. There was not much chance of getting a job, and many blind people had to beg in the streets.

Blind people were sometimes given jobs making baskets and brushes. This photograph of girls learning to be basket-makers was taken in the early 20th century.

This 16th-century drawing is one of the first pictures of someone wearing spectacles. Can you spot the monk with the glasses?

A great invention

Today, many people wear glasses, but for a long time, only a few people were lucky enough to own a pair. No one knows who invented glasses, but we do know that spectacles were first worn in Europe in the 13th century.

THINK ABOUT

Blind characters

Have you ever read a book with a blind character in it? In the past, many blind characters in books were not realistic at all. Sometimes authors made characters blind so that the reader would feel sorry for them. In *Treasure Island*, an old beggar is made to seem even more ugly and frightening because he is blind. What does this tell you about the way people reacted to blindness in the past?

Help for blindness

Every now and then, people see dramatic stories on the news about blind people suddenly regaining their sight. It sounds exciting, but it doesn't happen very often. However, doctors have become much better at stopping people's sight from getting any worse. Doctors can also help people make the most of the vision they have left.

What can we correct?

There are ways of helping people with poor sight. Many people wear glasses or contact lenses. Today, cataracts can be removed with an operation.

Another way of solving eye problems is by taking eye drops, which contain helpful drugs. Drops get rid of the liquid that can build up behind the eye and make it sore. They also clear up infections that can make the eye red.

Contact lenses are usually made from a type of plastic. The lens is placed carefully on the surface of the eye. People who wear contact lenses have to clean them every day.

Laser treatment

The retina is a sensitive part of the eye that can tear. Laser surgery can be used to treat this. A strong beam of light is directed into the eye and onto the damaged area. The laser joins the small tears with its powerful beam. Laser treatment can also help scars on the eye caused by diabetes. It doesn't cure the damaged parts, but it can stop the scars from getting any worse.

Sensory rooms

The world can be a frightening and mysterious place for partially-sighted children. Some children enjoy visiting a sensory room filled with relaxing music and bright, colorful lights. This helps them to use their sight better.

Laser surgery can be used to help people who are near-sighted or far-sighted.

This partially-sighted boy is able to see lots of colors and shapes in a sensory room.

(THINK ABOUT)

Helping yourself

Even if their sight can't be improved, people find ways of making the most of what they have left. Strong **magnifying glasses** help people to read, get around, or recognize friends. Sometimes people have to hold their heads in strange-looking positions to see clearly. You should never tease people like this who look different or move awkwardly. They are only trying to make the most of their sight.

At home

Blind children can do almost all of the things that their sighted brothers and sisters can do. They can play games, prepare meals, or help with the housework. As long as a blind child has the right help, he or she can join in almost anything that families do together.

Playing games

Many board games can be adapted for blind children to play by touch. There are balls with bells or beepers inside so that they can be heard as well as seen. And there are always games that don't need any equipment, such as truth or dare.

▲ Using her sense of touch, a blind woman peels potatoes for a meal. The more she practices, the easier the task will become.

In the kitchen

When blind people do everyday tasks, they use their other senses to make up for their lack of sight. If they are pouring a drink, they listen as the juice goes into the glass, or they simply stick their fingers in the top until something wet touches them. When they cut bread or spread butter, they can use one hand to make sure that the knife is straight. Blind people also easily learn to work the controls on appliances such as toasters.

Story time

Blind children have lots of books to choose from: large print books, books on tape, Braille books, and even Braille comics. Some books have raised, bumpy pictures so that blind readers can feel what the characters in the story look like.

▶ This blind boy and his sighted sister can read together because their book is in both Braille and ordinary print.

THINK ABOUT

Joining in

Blind children have the same interests as you. They enjoy listening to music, videos, and television programs, as well as just hanging out. As long as you give them a helping hand outside, they will be able to go wherever you and your friends go.

At school

A huge amount of students' schoolwork depends on eyesight. Students read books, look at computer screens, or watch their teacher carry out experiments. Blind and partially-sighted children need to use different methods to do the same kind of work.

Special schools

For a long time, people thought that the best way to teach blind children was to put them all together in special schools. These schools had special equipment—Braille books, writing machines, and maps with raised lines—and teachers trained to help blind children.

These days, more and more blind children go to local schools and learn with their sighted friends. There are still some very good special schools, but most people now agree that blind and sighted children should grow up together whenever possible so that they can learn from each other.

▶ A geography class in a school for blind children in 1908. The separate schools kept sighted students from learning more about blindness and made blind students feel isolated.

The Braille system

Braille is a system of raised dots that are combined to form all the letters of the alphabet, as well as punctuation such as commas and periods. Invented more than 150 years ago, Braille opened up the world of reading and writing to blind children. Braille is commonly used in books, but it is also used to make maps and diagrams.

◀ Blind people can read Braille with their fingers very fast with some practice.

A B C D E F G H I J K L M
N O P Q R S T U V W X Y Z

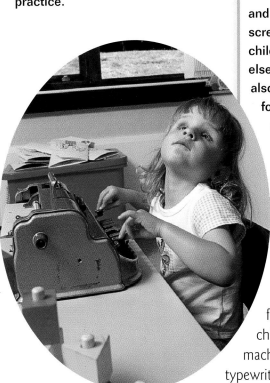

◢ This girl is learning to use a Braille typewriter in a special center for young blind children.

(THINK ABOUT)

Computers

Children with any kind of sight loss can use computers to work and play—just like you. There are computers that print extra-large letters or have a Braille display. Some computers have speech chips and can read out what's on the screen. This allows blind children to read what everyone else is reading, and they can also write their own reports for others to read. Blind children can be part of the class instead of having to study on their own.

Reading and writing

There are many ways to make schoolwork easier for blind children. Some children use special writing machines that look like typewriters and punch out Braille dots on thick paper. Children with some sight have books with extra-large print; magnifying glasses can also be used to make the print stand out more clearly. Blind children sometimes listen to books and lessons on tape.

Getting around

Anyone who has ever roller-skated in the park knows that a person has to think quickly and be aware of the people and objects around her. Blind people rely on the same skills of awareness to get around safely. They avoid accidents by using their common sense to determine where they are and what's going on around them.

New ways of getting around

In the past, blind people found it very difficult to move around on their own. It was only after World War I that doctors began to think about ways to help people who could not see. In the war, many soldiers had been blinded while fighting. They were still young and wanted to work and lead a normal life after the war. The two most successful ideas developed were the **cane** and the **guide dog**.

These soldiers were blinded by poison gas—a very dangerous weapon—in World War I.

The white cane

Canes were invented after World War I. People with poor sight had always used sticks to lean on, but canes also helped them to avoid obstacles. The canes were made of light metal and colored white so that they could be seen easily. Many blind people now use canes.

Guide dogs for the blind

Another good idea for helping blinded soldiers was to use dogs to lead them; it became so popular that soon blind people all over the world had guide dogs. A dog and its owner are trained to work together. The blind person has to be in control and the dog must know exactly what to do. Guide dogs are also sometimes called Seeing-Eye dogs.

▲ A blind boy learns to use a long cane. The cane's red bands show that the boy is deaf too.

THINK ABOUT

Finding the way

Imagine what it would be like to walk to school if you couldn't see. Could you figure out which way to go? How would you know when it was safe to cross the road? There is so much traffic on many roads that blind people need a lot of skill and confidence to go out alone. They listen carefully to the sounds around them, remember which way to turn, and always cross the road at marked crosswalks.

Out and about

The outside world is noisy and fast-paced. Sighted people just look at signs to find out which store is which or where a bus stop is, but blind people have a tougher time catching buses or finding their way to the library or grocery store.

Listening and remembering

Blind people have always found ways of moving around without much help. Some people can tell a lot from the **echo** of their feet on the pavement and learn to sense when they have reached an intersection or if they are near an obstacle such as a lamp post or bus shelter. Landmarks such as a set of railings or a park bench can help a blind person to remember a route and to figure out if he is going the right way.

A blind woman finds her way around a busy market. She has a long cane to help her, but her sense of direction is very important as well.

Crossing the road

There are many new ideas to help blind people. Some crosswalks beep to indicate when it's safe to cross. Pavement next to the crossing is often bumpy or rough to let blind people know it's a safe place to cross.

Traveling around

If a blind person wants to know which bus or train has arrived, often the best way is to ask other passengers. Clear and detailed announcements help too. In the future, there may be talking bus stops, shops, phone booths, and ticket machines that are **programmed** to provide important information to blind people.

This mailbox in France has Braille labels. Many public places are now using Braille signs.

The inside of this college for blind students has been carefully designed. It is brightly colored with tall windows to let in lots of light. Handrails along each wall help to guide people.

Inside buildings

There are many inexpensive things that can be done to help the blind move from place to place more easily. Architects could think more about **acoustics** in their buildings so that there aren't too many confusing echoes. Good lighting helps people who have some vision, and clear color **contrasts** can make it easier for them to see the difference between the walls and the floor.

THINK ABOUT

Lending a hand

Even with all these new ideas, there are still many times when you can give blind people a hand. It's usually best to let blind people take your arm while you walk slightly ahead, guiding them carefully past obstacles. Always be sure to ask first if help is needed, and then check how they want you to help them. They will know what makes them feel most comfortable.

Fun and games

Blind people enjoy sports and games just as much as sighted people and find ways of adapting sports to make them easier. For example, blind people can play ball games by putting a bell or rattle inside the ball. A blind person can't ride a bicycle, but he could ride a tandem bike with a sighted person in front.

All sorts of sports

Some sports are easier for the blind than most people think. Swimming can be fun for people who are totally blind because they are in an enclosed area with a wall around the pool that allows them to guide themselves. Anyone who enjoys swimming knows that sight is not really important since swimmers have their head under the water a lot of the time anyway. There are also blind athletes who take part in races by running alongside a sighted guide or having a "caller" at the end of the track who shouts out instructions.

Being blind does not stop some people from being athletes. This runner has a sighted guide who makes sure that he stays inside his lane.

Arts and crafts

A person doesn't need to have good eyesight to be an artist; many blind people enjoy all sorts of arts and crafts. Some people who can't see enough to paint try pottery-making or sculpture instead.

THINK ABOUT

Sports and hobbies

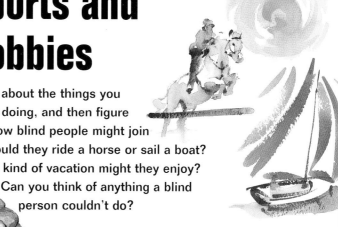

Think about the things you enjoy doing, and then figure out how blind people might join in. Could they ride a horse or sail a boat? What kind of vacation might they enjoy? Can you think of anything a blind person couldn't do?

This colorful sculpture was made by a blind artist using paper-mâché, clay, polystyrene, and tissue paper.

Putting on a show

Some blind people enjoy taking part in plays or dance productions; there are many blind theater groups that they can join. Blind actors learn their way around the stage the same way that they memorize the route to stores or the way around their house.

In this dance production, the dressed-up man in the middle is a blind actor. The other actors guide him around the stage, but they do it so cleverly that the audience often doesn't even realize he's blind.

Going to work

Just like sighted people, blind people want a job when they are adults. They often have the right skills, but many employers are afraid that a blind person won't be able to do the job well. This fear is why only about one in four blind people of working age in the United States and Great Britain has a job.

Working in radio

Roger Smith is a DJ with his own radio show; he works at a radio station at a college for blind people. He was determined that being blind would not stop him from having a job he enjoys.

Roger knows exactly where everything is in the studio, so he has no problems doing live radio shows.

Using computers

In the past, most people thought that the blind couldn't do complicated or difficult jobs. Today, blind people take on all kinds of different jobs. Computers have helped a lot by allowing blind people to read and write reports on their own.

Training to be a pilot

Although Ken Woodward was blinded in an accident, he now has a job in an office and has also trained as a pilot. He uses his other senses to help him fly, and he listens carefully to the instructions his co-pilot gives him through a headset.

In 1996, Ken flew around Great Britain to raise money for charity. Many people thought that a blind person couldn't fly a plane, but Ken proved them wrong.

This guide dog has been trained to guide its owner to work safely. A person should never distract a guide dog by feeding or petting it.

Being in charge

It takes a lot of confidence and ability to run a company. The blind woman shown at the left has her own computer business and travels to work with the help of her guide dog.

THINK ABOUT

Careers

Think about a job you would like to have. Could blind people do it? Maybe they couldn't drive a taxi, but what about operating the radio to tell drivers where to go? They might not be able to play football, but what about looking after injured players and helping them train as they recover? Blind people can do all kinds of jobs if they are given the chance.

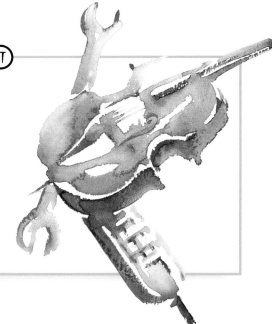

Amazing inventions

Scientists, inventors, and ordinary people are always thinking of ideas to help blind people. Some of these inventions are very expensive, such as computers that talk and machines that read and write. Other ideas are simple and inexpensive, such as putting different-shaped buttons on a shirt or dress to tell a blind person what color it is.

Pouring a drink

One man had a good idea when his father became blind. He noticed that his father had trouble pouring a cup of tea, so he invented a **gadget** that hangs on the edge of a cup and makes a beeping noise when the hot liquid nears the top.

Pouring boiling water could be very dangerous without one of these gadgets. They are brightly colored so that partially-sighted people can see them better.

Telling time

Everyone needs to be able to tell time. **Tactile** watches are designed to help blind people tell time by touch. There are also watches that speak or have extra-big numbers.

◀ The lid of this tactile watch lifts up so that a blind person can feel the hands and the bumps next to each number.

Hundreds of inventions

Many ordinary objects are adapted for blind people to use. Weight scales, microwave ovens, and thermometers have all been designed to speak. There are all kinds of helpful gadgets for the kitchen, such as measuring cups with raised markings and a metal disk that is placed in the bottom of a pan and rattles when the liquid boils.

▲ This telephone has very large buttons so that people who are partially-sighted can find numbers easily.

THINK ABOUT

New ideas

Think of ways to redesign your favorite games so that a blind friend could play them with you. What would need to be changed? Maybe the board and the pieces could be bigger. Maybe the dots on dominoes could be raised or the chutes and ladders on a board could be bumpy so that a person could feel them. You might try using pegs that fit into holes in a board to keep score.

Being a success

Most people think that it must be difficult for the blind to lead a normal life; they often don't realize how much people without sight can do. This type of thinking means that blind people have to work hard to persuade others to give them a chance. But through history, blind people have achieved many great things.

Louis Braille (1809-1852)

Louis Braille lost his sight in an accident at the age of three. He invented the Braille system when he was 15 years old, but because he was blind and only a child, no one took much notice. It was only after his death that people realized how brilliant his idea was.

▲ In this advertisement, Louis Braille is remembered as a great man who gave blind people the chance to read.

Helen Keller (1880-1968)

Helen Keller became blind and deaf at the age of two after suffering from **German measles**. At first she could not communicate at all, but with a lot of patience, she learned to speak and to read Braille. She became a great writer and teacher and gave talks all over the world to raise money for deaf and blind people.

◀ Helen Keller found that she could tell what people were saying by feeling their faces and lips as they spoke. This isn't something that blind people normally do, but for her it was the only way to share a conversation.

Stevie Wonder (1950-)

Stevie Wonder, who has been blind since birth, is one of the world's most famous musicians. He made his first record when he was 10 years old, and since then he has written and performed music all over the world. He sings and plays the harmonica, piano, organ, and drums.

David Blunkett (1947-)

David Blunkett, the man who runs all the schools in Great Britain, is blind. He went to a school for blind children and later became the leader of the city council in the same town. He is now a leading government official, and he and his guide dog are often seen on television.

 Stevie Wonder in concert. He often helps to raise money for other blind people.

David Blunkett and his guide dog Lucy, who stays with him all day at work.

THINK ABOUT

Fame

Have you heard of any other famous blind people? Try to learn about more blind achievers and how they overcame problems to succeed.

Looking to the future

One hundred years ago, many blind children didn't go to school, and not many of them found jobs. There were only a few Braille books and no guide dogs, and those who dared to go outside held on to someone's arm or leaned on a stick. A lot has changed over the last century. So what can we expect from the next 100 years?

Improving eyesight

Blindness will probably never disappear entirely, but treatment for eye problems is improving all the time. There are some exciting new developments such as a **bionic** eye that would **transmit** what we see straight to the brain, skipping over the part of the eye or the nerve that is damaged. But this technology may be a long way off.

Mobility aids

Some blind people now use special laser and **radar** equipment to help them move around. These devices, which are held or worn like glasses, give out sound messages about obstacles in front of the person. A machine that acts as a mechanical guide dog is also being developed. It would tell the blind person where obstacles are so they could be avoided.

Many aids are now being developed to guide people around. But do you think many blind people would want to carry all of this equipment?

This headband is part of a device called a Sonic Pathfinder. It gives out signals to tell blind people if there is an object in front of them. It can't guide people though, so they would need to use a guide dog or a cane as well.

Computerized help

More blind and sighted people have computers at home than ever before. People can go shopping, get books from the library, or even take classes without having to leave the house. The Internet allows people to find all kinds of information. Both blind and sighted people will be able to do even more using computers and the Internet in the future.

Many blind children enjoy reading stories or looking at pictures on computer. The print is very big, and sometimes the pictures move.

THINK ABOUT

Ways to help

Everyone can do his or her part to help blind people. It would help if signs were written in Braille or put on tape, and if people didn't leave bicycles and cars on sidewalks. People should remember that being blind means that people can't see—it doesn't mean that they can't think. Inventors and scientists help blind people a lot, but families and friends can do even more.

Glossary

acoustics How sound is heard. In a building with bad acoustics, sounds can either echo around the room or be muffled. This confuses blind people who need to hear clear sounds to figure out where things are.

adapted Changed or improved for a special reason.

AIDS A disease called acquired immune deficiency syndrome. AIDS destroys white blood cells in the body so it cannot protect itself against diseases. Some diseases affect the eyes.

bionic Something that has had a natural part replaced with electronic equipment.

Braille A system of writing invented by a Frenchman named Louis Braille. Each letter, made up of a simple pattern of raised dots, is read by touch. Some blind people can't read Braille because their sense of touch is not good enough.

cane A long stick that blind people move from side to side as they walk. It helps them avoid obstacles in front of them. The safest and most useful cane, called the long cane, can be folded up when it is not being used.

cataracts A clouding of the eye's lens. Some cataracts are so bad that the person can hardly see at all. An operation can break up the cataract and wash it out of the eye. Doctors can also replace the damaged lens with a special plastic lens.

contrasts When two colors are contrasts, they are very different from each other, so each color stands out clearly. Yellow and black are contrasting colors, but yellow and white are not.

diabetes A disease that stops the body from controlling the level of sugar in the blood. This causes problems such as tiredness, thirstiness, and blurred vision. People with diabetes must get treatment or their eyesight could be permanently damaged.

echo A sound that bounces back. Echoes are loudest in a building or a tunnel. A person walking along a quiet hallway at school will hear the echo of his footsteps. Blind people listen to echoes to figure out where they are—if they are in a big or a small room, for example. Blind people are aware of echoes outside in the street as well.

far-sighted An eye condition that makes it difficult for some people to see objects close to them.

gadget A small mechanical device or piece of equipment.

German measles A disease also called rubella that causes a sore throat and a skin rash. In the past, many children were born blind and deaf because their mothers had German measles when they were pregnant. Today, all girls are given a vaccination (injection) to protect them against this disease.

glaucoma An eye disease that is caused when watery liquid inside the eye presses too hard against the nerve and damages it, causing the person to lose some sight or even become blind.

guide dog A dog trained to lead a blind person around. These dogs, which make good companions as well as helpful aids, are also sometimes called Seeing-Eye dogs.

laser A very thin and powerful beam of light. The light does not spread out like the light from a lamp or a flashlight, so it can be directed precisely onto a certain point. Lasers can also be used in equipment that warns people of obstacles ahead; the laser bounces off of objects and sends a signal back to the blind person.

lens The clear part of the eye through which a person sees. Images are then directed onto the retina.

magnifying glass A lens that a person looks through to see a larger image of something. Magnifying glasses are useful to partially-sighted people for reading or doing other things such as sewing.

near-sighted An eye condition that makes it difficult for some people to see objects that are far away. Near-sightedness is very common and often becomes worse as people grow older.

nerve A tiny, thin connection that carries messages to the brain from all parts of the body.

partially-sighted Able to see some things but not very clearly. People who are partially-sighted can see more than people who are truly blind.

programmed Specially designed to do a certain thing. Talking bus stops of the future would be specially programmed by computer to read out schedules and announce the arrival of a bus.

radar A piece of equipment that makes a sound when it picks up signals from an object. The blind person can then avoid the obstacle ahead. Radar devices can be very expensive.

retina An area in the back of the eye that it is very sensitive to light. Images of what a person sees are carried from the retina to the brain, which then makes sense of the images.

tactile Something that can be touched or is related to the sense of touch.

transmit To send or pass on from one place to another.

Useful addresses

For more information about blindness, contact these organizations or visit their web sites.

American Council of the Blind
1155 15th Street NW, Suite 720
Washington, DC 20005
http://www.acb.org/

American Foundation for the Blind
11 Penn Plaza, Suite 300
New York, NY 10001
http://www.afb.org/

Associated Services for the Blind
919 Walnut Street
Philadelphia, PA 19107
http://www.libertynet.org/asbinfo/

Blind Childrens Center
4120 Marathon Street
Los Angeles, CA 90029
http://www.blindcntr.org/

The Canadian National Institute for the Blind
1929 Bayview Avenue
Toronto ON M4G 3E8
http://www.cnib.ca/

Guide Dog Foundation for the Blind
371 East Jericho Turnpike
Smithtown, NY 11787
http://www.guidedog.org/

Helen Keller International
90 Washington Street, 15th floor
New York, NY 10006
http://www.hki.org/

National Federation of the Blind
1800 Johnson Street
Baltimore, MD 21230
http://www.nfb.org/

National Industries for the Blind
(job opportunities for the blind)
1901 N Beauregard Street
Suite 200
Alexandria, VA 22311
http://www.nib.org/

Index